Your Dad Misses You

Support and Hope for Families Affected by Suicide

By Wayne Decker · Illustrated by Courtney Robertson

ISBN: 979-8-9903416-0-9 (Paperback)
ISBN: 979-8-9903416-1-6 (Hardcover)

Library of Congress Control Number: 2024906159

Any references to historical events, real people, or real places are used fictitiously. Names, characters, and places are products of the author's imagination.

Written by Wayne Decker
Illustrated by Courtney Robertson
Book design by Misty Black Media, LLC
Edited by Lor Bingham

The National Suicide Prevention Hotline 1-800-273-8255 or 988

First printing edition 2025

Chubbuck, Idaho

This book is dedicated to our daughter KyLee.

Love,

Mom. Dad.

Payton. and Adalyn

As your dad, I knew you had struggles here on Earth, but that day they were too much to bear.

The last memory I have of you overwhelms me with pain and guilt. You walked past me with a determined look on your face, your eyes locked straight ahead. I didn't know the severity of that moment, but now I do.

I feel pain inside, knowing I should have said something or reached out to you, possibly breaking your focus, instead I sat and said nothing, ultimately a choice I must now live with.

I'm lost, mentally in a place I've never been, not knowing where to turn. I'm holding this grieving pain deep inside, trying to act strong, holding in my emotions, falling into a seemingly never-ending depression fueled by guilt and the loss of my child.

I remember the day I brought you home and how excited our family was. As you got into your teenage years, things started to change. You began pushing me away, closing the door between us. I hardly got to see you. At home you were rarely happy, but around your friends you were the life of the party. I was envious of those that got to experience the happy you.

When I'm home
alone, I go to your
room where time
stands still and
everything is where it was
the day you left. I sit on the
edge of your bed and my
emotions pour out. I talk to you
as if you're sitting next to me. I
don't talk to anyone else because
they can't relate, they don't
understand. I tell you how much I
love you and how much I miss you. I talk
about my day and whatever else
comes to mind. I let you know there is not
a day that goes by that I don't think
about you.

I know your spirit's still here;
you're finding little ways to
show me. The times I've heard
wind chimes blowing in the
wind or have a butterfly land
on my arm. I feel a calmness
come over me.

The time I heard your voice whisper from behind me into my ear, you didn't say much, just one word, "Dad", it was so real, so clear, so distinct, I turned around expecting to see you standing there. I knew you were doing these things to help comfort me, letting me know I will be OK.

You come to me in dreams that are unlike any I've had before, so real, so vivid, so aware. In these dreams I'm amazed because I know you are gone and yet you're standing there talking to me. In one dream I even asked your brother how long you have been standing there. You smiled as you told me you were here to help someone. I noticed the happiness on your face and in your voice, something that was absent before.

After your passing it felt like you were so far away, but you have shown me you're still so very near. Watching over us, lifting us up, pushing us along. I've started opening up and talking to people again at work, telling family about my experiences and emotions. Nobody will fully understand what I'm going through and that's OK.

My broken heart will never fully heal, but knowing you'll be by my side makes each day more bearable.

When the time comes and we are all free of our earthly struggles we will be together again and I know you will say to me, "Dad, I missed you, now let me show you around."

About the Author:

Wayne is married to his beautiful wife Sabrina and has 3 children. He finds writing to be therapeutic and has seen the power words can have on people's lives. He hired on with Union Pacific Railroad in 2003. He also loves to spend time working on his garden railroad and just being outdoors.

About the Illustrator:

Courtney recently settled in Salmon, Idaho, where she lives with her dogs, Zeke and Moose, and someone who makes the quiet life feel just right.

www.ingramcontent.com/pod-product-compliance
Lightning Source LLC
Chambersburg PA
CBHW041530120626
46551CB00018B/2643